More! Instant Bible Lessons for Preschoolers

I Praise Jesus

Pamela J. Kuhn

These pages may be copied.

Permission is granted to the buyer of this book to
photocopy student materials in this book for
use with Sunday school or Bible teaching classes.

An imprint of Rose Publishing, Inc.
Carson, CA
www.Rose-Publishing.com

To my first born grandson, Ethan Chandler Clemens:
Thanks for making me a grandma and for climbing on my knee to let me read you stories. I want you to learn the wonderful love of Jesus as you grow strong, and enjoy the great stories in the Bible. I love you, Mawmaw.

MORE INSTANT BIBLE LESSONS FOR PRESCHOOLERS: I PRAISE JESUS
©2009 Pamela J. Kuhn, fifth printing
ISBN 10: 1-58411-069-4
ISBN 13: 978-1-58411-069-9
RoseKidz® reorder# R36855
RELIGION / Christian Ministry / Children

RoseKidz®
An imprint of Rose Publishing, Inc.
17909 Adria Maru Lane
Carson, CA 90746
www.Rose-Publishing.com

Cover Illustrator: Tammie Lyon
Interior Illustrator: Hallie Gillett

Unless otherwise noted, scriptures are from the *Holy Bible: New International Version* (North American Edition), ©1973, 1978, 1984 by the International Bible Society. Used by permission of Zondervan Bible Publishers.

Scriptures marked CEV are from the New Testament of the Contemporary English Version: © The American Bible Society 1995. Published under license from Thomas Nelson Publishers. Used by permission.

Scriptures marked NIrV are taken from HOLY BIBLE, NEW INTERNATIONAL READER'S VERSION®, Copyright 1995, 1996, 1998 by International Bible Society. Used by permission of Zondervan. All rights reserved.

Printed in the United States of America

Contents

Introduction

Wecome to *I Praise Jesus*, a book packed full with useful lesson activities for your preschoolers. You'll find the lively Bible stories and kid-friendly activities make it easy to teach about all the reasons why we praise Jesus, such as His peace, miracles, comfort and promise of heaven. Engage your students with active games and songs, set to familiar melodies, along with age-appropriate puzzles and worksheets. You'll find clear directions and lists of materials for the crafts and snacks, so you'll always be ready to go.

Each of the first eight chapters includes a Bible story, memory verse and numerous activities to help reinforce the lessons about the ways we praise Jesus. An additional chapter contains projects that can be used anytime throughout the study or at the end to review the lessons. Teacher aids, including bulletin board ideas and discussion starters, are sprinkled throughout the book.

The most exciting aspect of the *More! Instant Bible Lessons for Preschoolers* series is its flexibility. You can easily adapt these lessons to a Sunday School hour, a children's church service, a Wednesday night Bible study, a Christian school classroom or family home use. And, because there is a variety of reproducible ideas from which to choose, you will enjoy creating a class session that is best for your group — whether large or small, beginning or advanced, active or studious.

This book is written to add fun and uniqueness to learning about the reasons why we praise Jesus. Teaching children is exciting and rewarding, especially when you successfully share God's Word and its principles with your students. *More! Instant Bible Lessons for Preschoolers* will help you accomplish that goal. Blessings on you as your students explore why they praise Jesus.

How to Use This Book

Each chapter begins with a Bible story for you to read to your class, followed by discussion questions. Then, use any or all of the activities in the chapter to help drive home the message of that lesson. Each activity is tagged with one of the icons below, so you can quickly flip through the chapter and select the projects you need. Simply cut off the teacher instructions on the pages and duplicate as desired.

craft   finger play   teacher help   bulletin board   activity

puzzle   action song   song   game   snack

Chapter 1
I Praise Jesus for His Example

 Memory Verse

I have set the example.
John 13:15 CEV

Story to Share
Watch Me Grow

To Mary, the trip from Nazareth to Bethlehem seemed like it would never end. But the trip was necessary. The king's law required the people to go back to the land where they were born so they could be taxed.

Clip, clop, clip clop. The donkey's feet moved in rhythm and bounced Mary as she rode him. Joseph walked by her. He smiled when she glanced at him.

"Almost there," he said cheerfully to his pregnant wife.

But when Joseph and Mary finally reached the town, they found there were no hotel rooms to rent. Finally an innkeeper offered his stable to the young couple. Joseph spread some clean hay on the floor for his wife, then covered it with his coat. Mary was thankful for the soft bed.

A little while later, Joseph made another bed, but this one was in the manger, where the animals ate. He again placed clean hay in the bed and covered it with a cloth. When Jesus was born, Mary gently placed her new son in the bed.

Mary and Joseph knew their son was special. They knew God had sent His Son into the world to be the Messiah – to save people from sin.

Jesus grew like other babies. He turned over, He crawled, He walked and then He ran! Jesus ate the good foods His mother prepared for Him. He played with His friends, and did His chores.

Jesus' earthly father, Joseph, was a carpenter. Jesus loved to watch him work in his shop.

"Let me feel it, Daddy," Jesus would say as Joseph sanded a board. Joseph would stand back and let Jesus feel the smooth wood he planned to use for a table. When Daddy said it was time to clean up, Jesus ran to get the broom with a smile on His face, happy to be helping.

Just like you are growing, Jesus grew healthy, strong, obedient and wise. Jesus is a good example for us.

— Based on Luke 2:1-7

 **Discussion Questions**

1. You probably were born in a hospital. Where was Jesus born? (stable)
2. How can you grow strong like Jesus? (eat healthy foods, run and play, be happy and obedient)

craft

What You Need
- duplicated page
- card stock
- baby food jars
- water
- baby-themed confetti
- glitter
- glue gun
- glue

What to Do
1. Before class duplicate the lid circle to card stock and cut out one for each child.
2. Fill each jar almost full with water.
3. Give each child several pieces of confetti to put in the water. Allow the children to shake glitter into their jars, too.
4. Keeping the glue gun out of the children's reach, run a rim of hot glue around the tops of each jar. Tightly screw the lid on each jar.
5. Give each child a circle to glue on the top of his or her jar.

His Example

Glitter Celebration Shaker

What To Say

Let's turn our shakers upside down. The world was sinful and needed a Savior. God gave us a tiny baby who would be the Savior of the world. Now we turn our shakers right side up and praise Jesus! Let's say, "Happy Birthday, Jesus." Jesus was a cheerful, willing helper when He was a boy. He obeyed His parents and was kind to His sisters and brothers. Jesus was a good example. Let's turn our shakers upside down and say, "I want to be a good example like Jesus!"

Praise Kazoo

Celebrate, celebrate,
Celebrate Christ's birth.
Cows and sheep sang Him
to sleep,
In quiet Bethlehem.

Celebrate, celebrate,
Celebrate the Child,

He was loving, kind
and good,
Helping cheerfully.

Celebrate, celebrate,
Celebrate God's Son.
He was a good example,
I want to be like Him.

Celebrate!

I have set the example. John 13:15

song

What You Need
- duplicated page
- wax paper
- tape
- crayons
- paper towel tubes

What to Do
1. Cut the paper towel tubes into 8-inch sections, one per child. Cover one end of each tube with wax paper and tape in place. Make a ¼" hole in the side of each tube. Duplicate a kazoo wrap for each child.
2. Allow the children to color their wraps.
3. Assist the children in taping the wraps snuggly around the tubes.
4. Instruct the children to blow in the open ends of the kazoos (make sure each child's name is on his or her kazoo for sanitary reasons). Sing the song to the tune of "Jingle Bells" while the children play their kazoos.

His Example

Clothespin Review

What You Need
- duplicated page
- crayons
- glue
- clothespins
- paper plates

What to Do

1. Duplicate and cut out a game board and hearts, one set per child.
2. Allow the children to color their game boards.
3. Instruct the children to color one heart for each color: blue, green, red, yellow, purple.
4. Assist in gluing the game board to the paper plate and a heart to five clothespins.
5. Retell the story on page 7. As each character or object is introduced, tell the children to clip the colored hearts to the game board, according the directions at right.

His Example

What To Say

Clip the yellow heart to Mary, Jesus's mother.
Clip the blue heart to Joseph, Jesus's earthly father.
Clip the red heart to the stable where Jesus was born.
Clip the purple heart to the animals from the stable.
Clip the green heart to God's Son, Jesus.

Snacks from the Stable

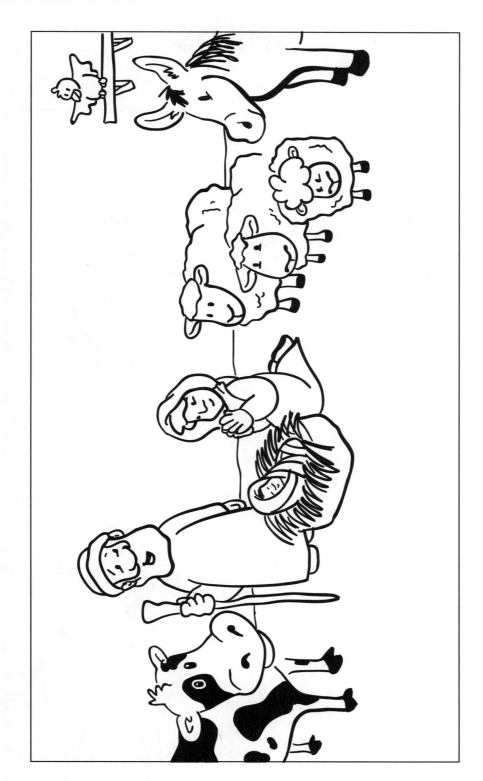

snack

What You Need
- duplicated page
- cups
- milk
- large marshmallows
- gummy worms
- wax paper

What to Do
1. Before class, duplicate the stable picture. Allow the children to color the picture.
2. Give each child a square of wax paper to cover the stable picture.
3. Instruct the children to place a cup of milk over the animal that gives us milk.
4. Give each child large marshmallows to place over the lambs.
5. Give each child a gummy worm to "feed" to the bird.
6. Now enjoy the stable snack!

Look at the happy stable animals. They were happy to share their home with baby Jesus. When you share your toys and home with others, you are like the stable animals. When you share, Jesus is happy, too.

His Example

puzzle

What You Need
- duplicated page
- crayons
- plastic sandwich bags

What to Do
1. Duplicate and cut out a sequence card set for each student.
2. Allow the children to color the cards.
3. Supply plastic sandwich bags for storage.
4. Explain that you will call out a sequence in which the children should place their cards. Look at each student's cards. If they are correct, say, "Jesus is born!" Quietly assist those who need help putting their cards in order.

Continued on next page...

His Example

Stable Sequence Cards

I have set the example.
John 13:15

puzzle

Continued from previous page...

What to Say

1. An animal that moos, one that is fluffy like cotton and a tiny baby.
2. The animal that carried Mary to Bethlehem, the place where Jesus was born.
3. God's Son, an animal that gives milk and Jesus's mother.
4. A home for animals, Jesus's parents and Jesus.
5. An animal that has feet which say "clip clop," Baby Jesus and the animal that says, "Baaa."

His Example

craft

What You Need
• duplicated page
• card stock
• gauze strips
• heart stickers

What to Do
1. Duplicate baby Jesus to card stock for each child.
2. Give each child a 12" piece of gauze to wrap around baby Jesus.
3. Say, "God loved us so much that He sent His Son to earth as a tiny baby. God sent Jesus to show us how to live."
4. As you give each child a heart sticker to put on the soft cloths, say, "God loved (child's name here)."

His Example

Wrapped in Love

Watch Me Move Exercise

game

What You Need
• duplicated page

What to Do

1. Practice the movements before class so you are ready to do them with the children.
2. After the children learn the movements, try speeding up the verse and actions for fun.

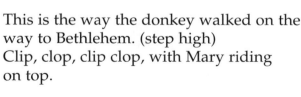

This is the way the donkey walked on the way to Bethlehem. (step high)
Clip, clop, clip clop, with Mary riding on top.

This is the way Joseph walked, all along the way. (march in place)
Step, step, step, step, Caesars' law was kept.

This is the way angels sang, announcing Jesus' birth. (open mouth wide)
La, la, la, la, the angels shepherds saw.

This is the way Mary rocked little baby Jesus. (rock back and forth)
Hush, hush, little boy, rocking with great joy.

This is the way Jesus swept up Joseph's wood shavings. (sweeping motions)
Sweep, sweep, sweep, sweep, all of them into a heap.

His Example

15

Just Like Me

craft

What You Need
- duplicated page
- crayons

What to Do
1. Duplicate a worksheet for each child.
2. Instruct the children to match the pictures of Jesus on the left to a corresponding picture on the right, drawing a line to the modern child doing the same action.
3. Allow the children to color the pictures.

What to Say
What kinds of things do you do for play time that Jesus might have done? (told riddles and played ball, hopscotch, and board games) How was Jesus a good example for us? God wants us to try to be like Jesus.

His Example

I have set the example. John 13:15

Chapter 2
I Praise Jesus for His Peace

Memory Verse

My peace I give you.
John 14:27

Story to Share
We're Going to Drown!

"This has been a busy day," Peter said to Jesus. "You have been teaching and healing for hours."

Jesus nodded His head wearily.

"Come," Peter urged Him. "Let's go for a ride in my boat."

Jesus and His disciples entered the boat, thankful for the promise of a quiet ride. Before Peter even picked up his oar to begin to row, Jesus was asleep, curled up in the corner of the boat.

It was getting toward evening, but Peter noticed that the sky seemed darker than usual. The waves began picking up speed and strength. The wind howled eerily.

The disciples looked at each other.

"There's a storm brewing!" Andrew yelled at Peter.

"It's too late to get back to shore in time to miss the storm," Peter yelled back.

Just then, a wave crashed into the boat and water sprayed on their clothes. The waves got fiercer and the wind stronger. The disciples became more frightened as the minutes passed. All through the storm, Jesus slept, exhausted from His day.

Scared, Thomas shook Jesus awake.

"Jesus," he called over the noise of the wind. "Save us, Jesus. We're going to drown."

Jesus rubbed His eyes and looked at the storm.

"Why are you afraid? Where's your faith?" He asked. Then Jesus stretched out His arms, and with His face turned toward the heavens said, "Peace. Be calm."

Instantly, the wind quieted, the waves became soft and gentle and the sky lightened. Jesus brought peace to a stormy night.

The disciples stared at Jesus. "Even the storms obey His voice," James said.

— Based on Matthew 8:23-27

Discussion Questions

1. Who was with the disciples when they were scared? (Jesus)
2. Are you ever afraid? Who is with you when you are? (Jesus)

Night Time Poster

craft

What You Need
- duplicated page
- black construction paper
- star stickers
- glue
- yarn
- hole punch
- yellow crayons

What to Do
1. Duplicate a moon and poem for each child.
2. Punch two holes at the top of each sheet of construction paper and tie yarn through the holes to create a hanger.
3. Allow the children to color the moons. Have them glue the moons in the centers of their black papers.
4. Give the children star stickers to stick around their moons.
5. Instruct the children to glue the poem to the bottom center of the posters.

Starry star light,
Starry star bright,
Jesus is with me in the night.

My peace I give you. John 14:27

Are you ever afraid at night? Hang your poster in your room to remind you that Jesus is watching over you. He will keep you safe.

His Peace

18

Rocking in the Storm

Oh when my boat,
Oh when my boat,
Oh when my boat rocks
in the storm.
I will let Jesus be my captain,
When my boat rocks
in the storm.

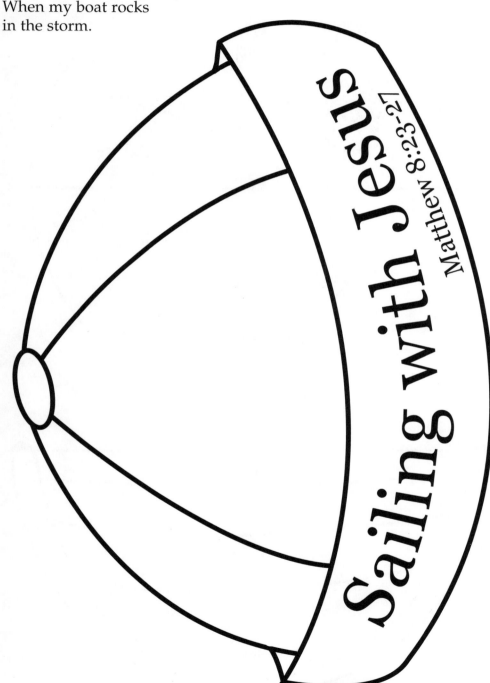

Sailing with Jesus
Matthew 8:23-27

song

What You Need
• duplicate page
• card stock
• white poster board
• stapler
• tape
• star stickers

What to Do
1. Duplicate the sailor hat to card stock and cut out one for each child.
2. Cut poster board in 3" wide strips (long enough to fit around a child's head).
3. Fit the strips to each child's head and staple the strips together. Staple the hat to the rim. Cover the staples with clear tape to avoid injury.
4. Give the children star stickers to decorate their hats.
5. Allow the children to wear their hats while they sing the "My Rockin' Boat" song to the tune of "When the Saints Go Marching In."

His Peace

Picture Wheel Boat

craft

What You Need
- duplicated page
- crayons
- paper fasteners

What to Do
1. Duplicate and cut out a boat and picture wheel for each child.
2. Allow the children to color the pictures and boats.
3. Assist the children in attaching the wheel to the boat with a paper fastener.

What to Say
Look at the disciples' faces. Do they look happy? (no, frightened) Let's turn our wheels. Now look at the disciples' faces. This time they are happy. That's because Jesus gives us peace. Let's say, "Peace, be calm," as we turn our wheels to show Jesus calming the storm.

His Peace

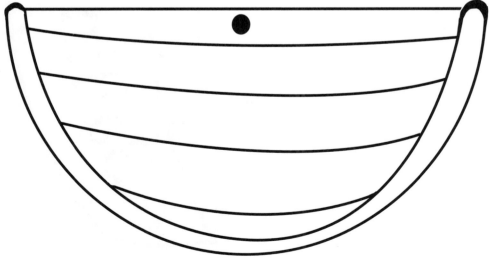

Who's Sleeping in the Boat?

Who is sleeping in the boat?

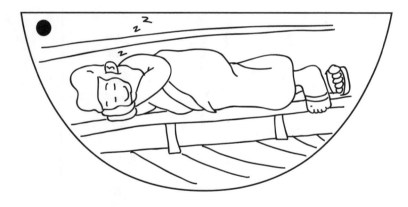

My peace I give you. John 14:27

What You Need
- duplicated page
- brown construction paper
- paper fasteners
- crayons

What to Do
1. Duplicate the two inside boat pieces for each child.
2. Trace the outside of the boat to brown construction paper.
3. Give each child the inside boats to color.
4. Assist the children in putting the three boat pieces together with a paper fastener on the left side.

What to Say
When Jesus came to earth as a man, He needed rest just like you and I do. But in heaven, God and His Son don't need sleep. We can call on Jesus for help any time.

His Peace

Jesus in the Boat

snack

What You Need
- duplicated page
- crayons
- clear, self-stick plastic
- pita bread
- peanut butter
- bananas
- fish stickers

What to Do
1. Duplicate a water mat for each child.
2. Pre-spread half of a pita with peanut butter for each child.
3. Allow the children to color the water mats blue and place the fish stickers in the water.
4. Assist the children in covering the mats with clear plastic.
5. Give each child a banana half to put to sleep in the pita boat.
6. Allow the children to rock the boat in the waves while they enjoy their snacks.
7. This mat can also be used with the Picture Wheel Boat on page 20.

His Peace

My peace I give you. John 14:27

What Does Not Belong?

What You Need
• duplicated page
• crayons

What to Do
1. Duplicate a worksheet for each child.
2. Instruct the children to look at the first box and draw a blue "X" on the object that does not belong in the water. Instruct the children to draw a green "X" on the object in the second box that do not belong in Sunday school, a red "X" on the object in the third box that does not belong at home, and an orange "X" on the object in the fourth box that does not belong in a zoo.

What to Say
Sometimes we have things in our hearts that don't belong there, such as jealousy, unkindness or untruthfulness. We need to ask Jesus to remove those things so we can have peaceful hearts.

His Peace

craft

What You Need
• duplicated page
• paper towel tubes
• glue
• aluminum foil
• clear tape

What to Do
1. Duplicate and cut out a microphone wrap for each child. Cut the paper towel tubes in half.
2. Allow the children to color the wraps.
3. Instruct each child to glue a wrap to a paper towel tube.
4. Give each child a square of foil. Show how to form a piece of foil into a ball, then wrap a smooth piece of foil over the ball. Assist with gluing the foil onto the top of the tube to make the microphone.
5. Allow the children to use their microphones as they pretend to be weather forecasters, giving the reports for when Jesus went out into the boat and for when the weather changed.

His Peace

Forecaster's Microphone

Jesus Is Captain of My Boat

Continued on next page...

bulletin board

What You Need
- duplicated pages
- blue spray paint
- lettering
- crayons
- camera

What to Do
1. Duplicate and cut out a boat for each child. Duplicate a set of weather patterns. Color them and cut them out.
2. Paint blue water and waves on the bulletin board. Attach lettering to the top of the board that reads "Jesus Is Captain of My Boat."
3. Give each child a boat to color.
4. Assist the children in printing their names on the boats.
5. Attach the boats to the waves on the board.
6. Each time you meet, allow the children to decide on the weather and attach the appropriate symbol to the sky on the board.

His Peace

Chapter 3
I Praise Jesus for His Miracles

 Memory Verse

See Jesus do a miracle.
Mark 3:10 NIrV

 Story to Share
Food for a Crowd

Jesus was tired. He had been preaching to crowds and healing the sick for many, many days.

"Let's get away and rest," Jesus told the disciples. So they got on their boat and sailed across the Galilee Sea.

But Jesus didn't get much time to rest. The people saw where He was heading and thousands followed Him because they knew He could heal them.

Jesus saw them. He saw that they needed healing and needed to be taught about God. Jesus spent much of the day talking to the crowd and healing those who needed it.

A small boy in the crowd saw Jesus doing these miracles. He saw a man who had a bad leg now walking around. He saw a blind woman looking with joy at her young son. He saw Jesus touch the ears of a man who couldn't hear – and then the man suddenly began to hear and talk!

This small boy knew Jesus was God's Son. When the disciples began looking for food for the people, he looked at his small lunch of five barley rolls and two small fish. It wasn't much, but he wanted to give it to Jesus – the miracle man!

Jesus took the boy's small lunch and thanked God for it. Then He told the disciples to pass the food around to all the people. The boy watched as the food turned into enough for everyone to eat – and there were 12 baskets left over. All from his tiny lunch!

The small boy ate until he was full, smiled to himself and whispered, "That's my Jesus!"

— Based on Mark 6:30-44

 Discussion Questions

1. Why did the little boy know Jesus could use his small lunch? (He saw Jesus perform many other miracles.)
2. Do you think Jesus still performs miracles? (yes—give an illustration from your life)

File Folder Story

craft

What You Need
- duplicated page
- felt
- crayons
- glue
- colored file folders
- envelopes
- fish stickers

What to Do
1. Duplicate and cut out a set of story pictures and a file label for each child. Also cut an 8" x 11" piece of felt for each child.
2. Allow the children to color the pictures.
3. Cut 1" squares of felt and instruct each child to glue a felt square to the back of each picture.
4. Allow the children to decorate the folders with fish stickers.
5. Instruct each child to glue an envelope (address side to folder) to the left side of the folder and a felt piece to the right side.
6. Tell the story on page 7, allowing the children to

Continued at right...

His Miracles

The Miracle of a Small Boy's Lunch

Continued from left...

arrange the pictures of Jesus's miracle inn the correct order, using the pictures and the folder. The felt backed pictures will adhere to the felt on the folder where the children place them. Encourage the children to retell the story to their family members and friends.

Count the Fish

3

2

5

4

1

not in Bible Times

puzzle

What You Need
- duplicated page
- crayons

What to Do
1. Duplicate a worksheet for each child.
2. Discuss the picture. Ask the children to find and circle the five things that would not have been found in Bible days.
3. Allow the children to color their pictures.

What to Say
Even though we don't live the same way as people in Bible days, we still praise Jesus like they did. Jesus still does miracles for us. Jesus will make us better when we are sick and He will provide food for us when we are hungry just like He did in Bible times.

His Miracles

30

Palette of Miracles

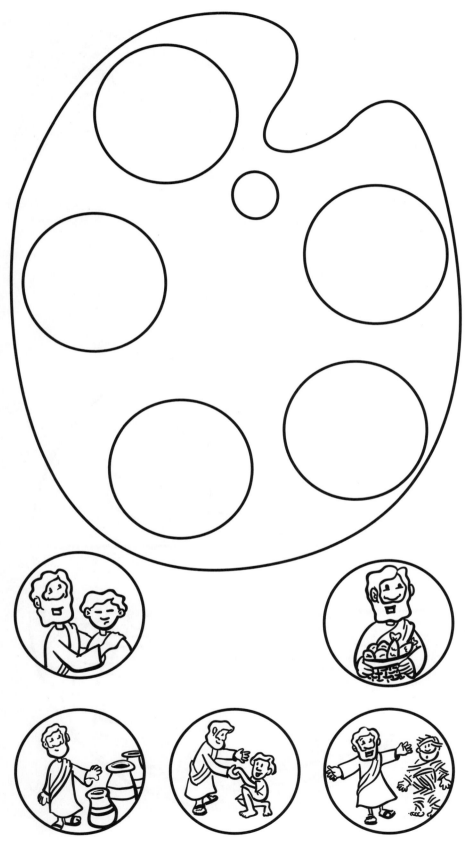

What You Need
- duplicated page
- white foam
- crayons
- glue
- paint brushes
- magnet

What to Do
1. Using the pattern, cut a palette from white foam for each child.
2. Duplicate and cut out a set of miracle pictures for each child.
3. Let the children color the pictures, one color for each picture.
4. Help the children glue the pictures to the palettes.
5. Instruct each child to glue a paint brush across his or her palette.
6. Help each child attach two magnets to the back.
7. Point to the pictures and discuss each of the miracles. Say, "Jesus's miracles are like colors – they're all special. We can celebrate Jesus's miracles!"

His Miracles

31

craft

What You Need
- duplicated page
- dessert-size paper plates
- curling ribbon
- hole punch
- glue

What to Do
1. Duplicate and cut out the patterns for each child.
2. Allow the children to color the patterns.
4. Assist the children in gluing the bread and the woven piece to the plate to form a basket.
5. Punch four holes around the bottom of each plate and at the mouth of each fish.
6. Cut lengths of curling ribbon. Assist the children in tying the fish to the bottoms of their plates. Go around and curl the ends of the ribbons with scissors.
6. Encourage the children to hang their Verse Baskets where they can be

Continued on next page...

His Miracles

Verse Basket

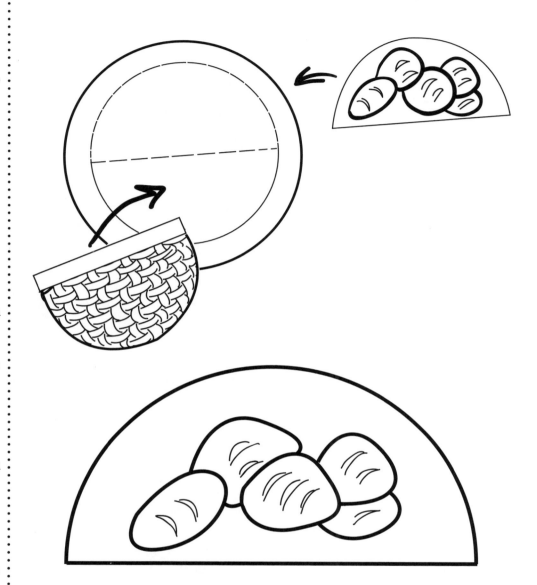

See Jesus

do a

miracle.

Mark 3:10

craft

Continued from previous page...
reminded of Jesus's miracles.

What to Say
Aren't you happy that Jesus will help us when we need Him, too?

His Miracles

song

What You Need
- duplicated page
- card stock
- crayons
- feathers
- glitter glue
- clear cellophane
- plastic drinking straws
- glue

What to Do
1. Duplicate two masks to card stock for each child. Cut out the eyeholes.
2. Allow the children to decorate one of the masks with crayons, feathers and glitter glue.
3. Give each child two 2" pieces of cellophane. Help the children glue the cellophane over the eyeholes on the backs of the masks.
4. Allow the children to glue their second masks to the backs of the decorated masks, sandwiching the cellophane between the two masks.
5. Staple a straw to

Continued at right...

His Miracles

The Miracle Worker Song

See Him, oh, see Him,
Oh see His miracles.
See Him, oh, see Him,
Oh see His miracles.
See Him, oh, see Him,
Oh see His miracles.
He's feeding everyone.

See me, oh, see me,
Oh see He made me.
See me, oh, see me,
Oh see He made me,
See me, oh, see me,
Oh see He made me.
I am His miracle.

Continued from left...

the right side of each mask. Cover the staples with clear tape to avoid injury. Show the children how to lift the mask to their face using the straw as a handle.
6. Sing the song to the tune of "Do Lord," encouraging the children to look through their masks when they sing "See Him" and then "See Me."

Fishy Snack

See Jesus do a miracle. Mark 3:10

4 tablespoons peanut butter
3 tablespoons powdered milk
1/2 cup crushed
crispy chocolate cereal
2 white chocolate chips

. . . snack . . .

What You Need
- duplicated page
- small bowls
- plastic spoons
- wax paper
- wet wipes
- fish snack ingredients (see left)
- white chocolate chips

What to Do
1. Duplicate a fish mat for each child.
2. Have the children wash their hands.
3. Give each child a square of wax paper to cover the fish mat.
4. Give each child a bowl with peanut butter and powdered milk in it and tell him or her to mix it thoroughly. Pour cereal in each bowl.
5. After the cereal is mixed completely, allow the children to form two fish each, using the patterns on the mat. Use white chocolate chips to make eyes.
6. Be prepared with the wet wipes!

His Miracles

craft

What You Need
- duplicated page
- letter envelopes
- glue
- wiggle eyes

What to Do
1. Duplicate nose, tongue and two ears for each child.
2. Give each child an envelope and instruct the children to seal their envelopes.
3. Allow the children to fold their envelopes in half (flap inside fold). Go around and cut a slit along the outer fold line.
4. Give the children the face pieces to glue in place. Allow the children to glue wiggle eyes on the faces.
5. Discuss what the little boy might have said when he told a friend about the miracle Jesus did with his lunch. Allow the children to pretend they are the boy and tell each other about Jesus' miracle, using the puppets.

His Miracles

Little Boy Puppet

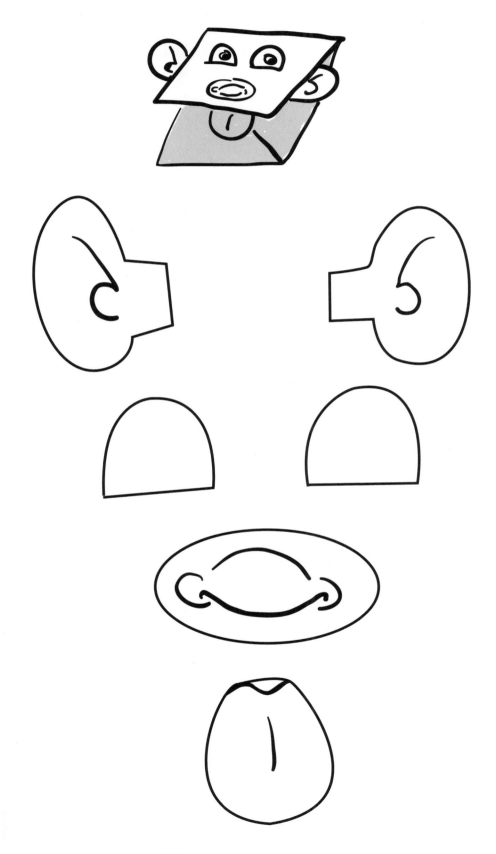

Chapter 4
I Praise Jesus for His Kindness

Memory Verse

The Lord is good.
Lamentations 3:25

Story to Share
She Needs Kindness

When Jesus was in Jerusalem, He spent much of His time teaching in the temple. The religious leaders hated Jesus and His message of love. They tried to trick Him into saying something wrong. But Jesus always said the right words.

One day while Jesus was teaching in the temple, the leaders came to Him, dragging a woman. The men shoved her until she fell at Jesus' feet. She was shaking with fear, and crying.

"Jesus," they said, "this woman was found with a man who was not her husband. The law says we should throw stones at her until she dies. What should we do?"

Jesus knew this woman had done wrong. He was sad when men and women didn't honor their marriages. But instead of answering the religious leaders, He bent down and wrote something in the dust with his finger.

The leaders thought Jesus wasn't listening to them, so they tried again. "What do You want us to do with her?"

Jesus pointed to what He had written in the dust. "Is there someone here who has never done anything wrong? If so, that person can throw the first stone."

The men looked at each another. They knew in their hearts that each one of them had done wrong. Silently, they all walked away, and Jesus was left alone with the woman. She was still kneeling in the dust, waiting for them to stone her.

"Woman," Jesus said kindly, "your accusers are gone. They did not punish you, and I will not either. I want you to go back to your husband and ask for his forgiveness. Make sure you never commit this sin again."

The woman lifted her tear-stained face to Jesus. She saw kindness in His eyes. "Thank You," she whispered. "Thank You."

— Based on John 8:1-11

Discussion Questions

1. Why did the leaders bring the woman to Jesus? (She had done wrong.)
2. Why did Jesus forgive her? (He is kind and willing to forgive instead of punish.)

craft

What You Need
- duplicated page
- glue
- party horns
- smiley stickers

What to Do
1. Duplicate and cut out a kindness strip for each child.
2. Show how to carefully stretch the curled end of a party horn and glue the kindness strip to it, leaving 1" of room at the tip.
3. Give each child a smiley sticker to place on the tip of the party horn, at the end of his or her kindness strip.
4. Allow the children to blow their horns as you sing "Jesus Loves Me." The second time you sing it, choose three "choir members" to sing with you. Give each child a chance to be a choir member while the others blow.

His Kindness

Party Horns of Kindness

K I n d n e s s	K I n d n e s s	K I n d n e s s

What did you put at the end of your kindness strip? That's right, a smiley face. Jesus was kind to the woman the religious leaders brought to Him. One way you can reach out in kindness is to smile. Try it, and see if someone smiles back at you!

Mr. Handy's Kindness

craft
. . . .

What You Need
- duplicated pages
- flesh-colored craft foam
- wiggle eyes
- markers
- craft sticks
- empty frosting tubs
- silver foil pieces
- spray cologne
- small bandages

What to Do
1. Duplicate and cut out a tub wrap and set of hands for each child.
2. Give each child a wrap to color. Allow the children to glue the wrap around the tubs.
3. Cut 3" circles from craft foam. Give a circle and two eyes to each child. Let each child glue the wiggle eyes to his or her foam face and draw a nose and smile.
4. Assist in gluing the faces to the backs of the tubs.
5. Give each child a hand set and three craft sticks. Allow the children to glue the hands to

Continued on next page...

His Kindness

39

craft

Continued from previous page...

the sticks.

6. Show how to attach the bandage to the injured hand and the foil to the candy kiss. Allow each child to spray some cologne on the flower.

7. Tell the children to put the sticks in the tub.

What to Say

Mr. Handy wants to help you be kind. Can you find the hand holding what you need when your friend gets hurt? (bandage) Which hand is holding what you need to give to someone who is sad? (a kiss) Which hand is holding what you can give your mommy or a sick neighbor? (flower) Smell your flower. When we spread kindness, it's like spraying perfume. It brings joy. God wants us to be kind.

His Kindness

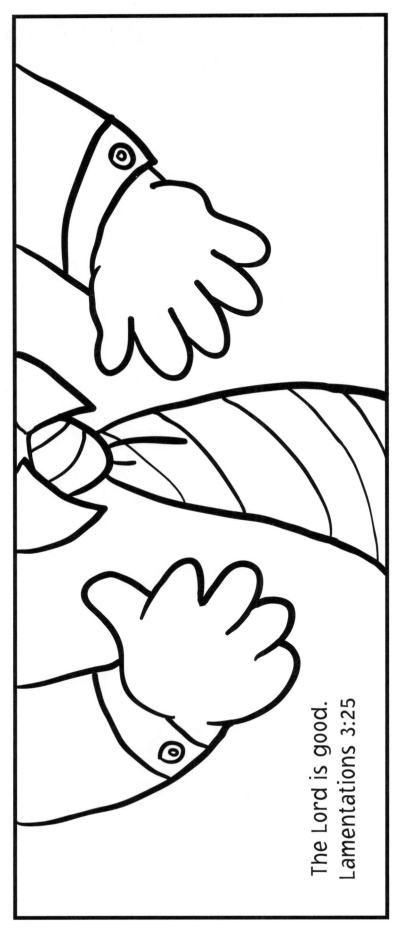

The Lord is good. Lamentations 3:25

Mouth of Kindness

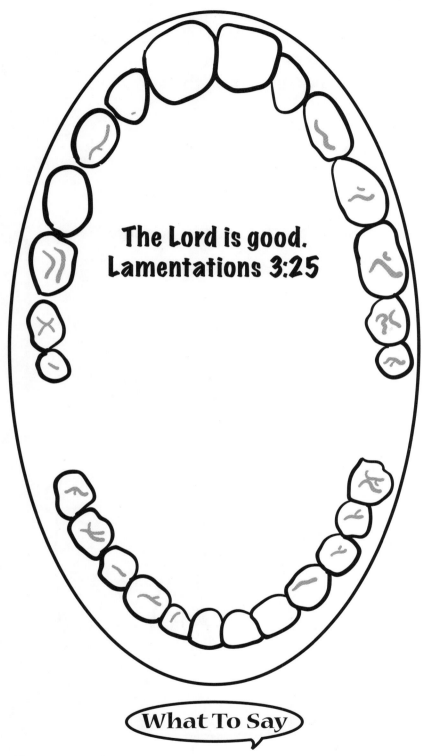

The Lord is good.
Lamentations 3:25

snack

What You Need
- duplicated page
- pink felt
- red crayons
- clear, self-stick plastic
- miniature marshmallows
- plastic sandwich bags
- strawberry whipped cream cheese
- glue

What to Do
1. Duplicate a mouth for each child. Cut a pink felt tongue for each child.
2. Allow the children to color the mouths red, leaving the teeth white.
3. Give each child a tongue to glue to his or her mouth.
4. Cover the mouths with clear plastic.
5. Give each child 20 marshmallows, one to put on each tooth. Spoon a bit of cream cheese on the tongue for dipping.
6. After the snack, wipe the mats clean to take home.

What To Say

Our mouths can be used to show kindness. Can you think of any way to show kindness with our mouths? We can smile at someone who looks sad. We can say "I love you" and "May I help you?" with our mouths. We can tell Jesus we want to be kind, just as He was. Let's thank the Lord for our food and ask Him to help us to always use our mouths kindly.

His Kindness

song

What You Need
- duplicated page
- craft sticks
- glue

What to Do
1. Duplicate a Bible woman for each child.
2. Allow the children to color the figures.
3. Instruct each child to glue a craft stick on the back of his or her figure.
4. Sing the "Do You Know" song to the tune of "Do You Know the Muffin Man?" Instruct the children to hold up their Bible women as they say the verse at the end.

His Kindness

Sin No More

Do you know what Jesus said,
What Jesus said, what Jesus said?
Do you know what Jesus said,
To the frightened woman?

Yes, I know what Jesus said,
What Jesus said, what Jesus said.
Yes, I know what Jesus said,
He said something kind.

Spoken: "Go and sin no more."

Find the Differences

puzzle

What You Need
- duplicated page
- crayons

What to Do
1. Duplicate a worksheet for each child.
2. Instruct each child to find five differences and circle them in blue.
3. Allow the children to color the pictures.

What to Say
There were many different times in the Bible when Jesus was kind. (Zacchaeus, Mary anointing Jesus' feet, woman at the well, etc.) Even though every situation isn't the same, you can know that Jesus' kindness never fails. He is always kind.

His Kindness

43

activity

What You Need
- duplicated page
- card stock
- crayons
- glue
- white board or chalkboard

What to Do
1. Duplicate shovels and letters to card stock and cut out a set for each child.
2. Let the children color their shovels.
3. Show how to fold the flap back on the shovel and glue the side and back edges to the back of the shovel to form a storage pocket.
4. Instruct the children to lay their letters on the table. Draw a "K" on the board. Say, "Find the letter 'K.' It's the first letter in the word 'kind.'"
5. Continue with the letters until the children have spelled "kind." Tell the children to point to the letters as you say each word of the verse.

His Kindness

Digging into God's Word

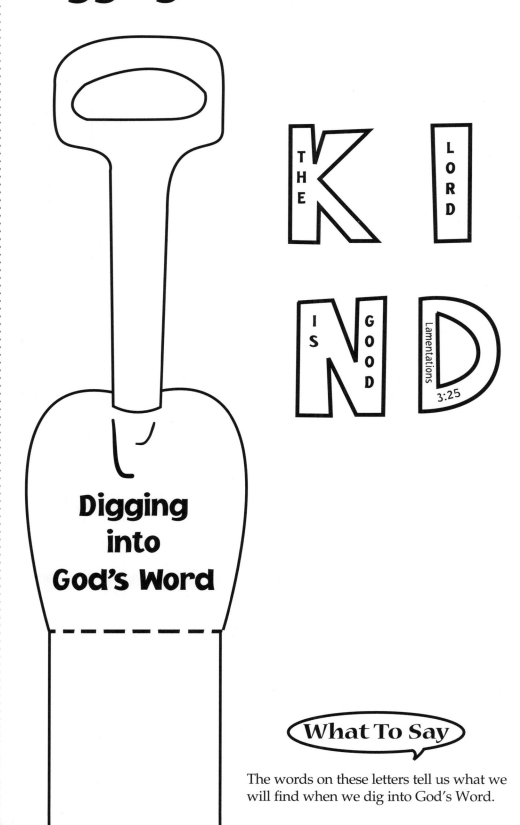

Digging into God's Word

THE **K** I N D LORD IS GOOD

Lamentations 3:25

What To Say

The words on these letters tell us what we will find when we dig into God's Word.

Kindness Certificate

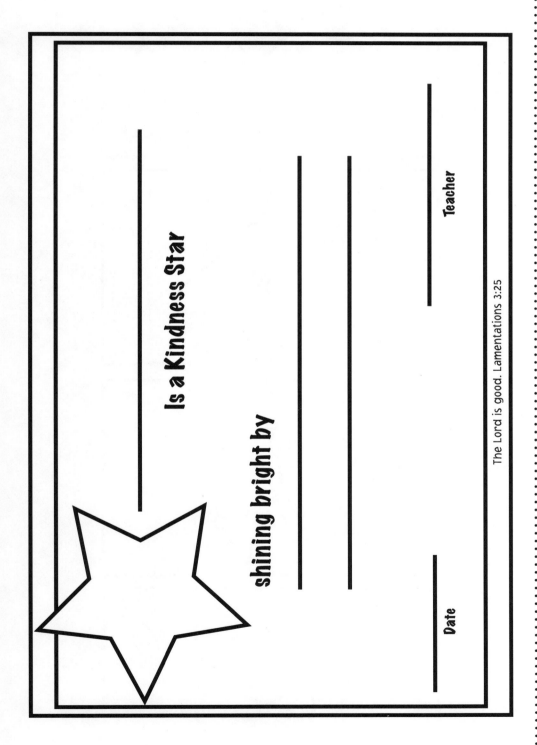

Is a Kindness Star

shining bright by

Teacher

Date

The Lord is good. Lamentations 3:25

teacher help

What You Need
- duplicated page
- star stickers

What to Do
1. Duplicate a Kindness Certificate for each child.
2. As you catch each child doing something kind, record it on a certificate.
3. Allow the children to decorate their certificates with star stickers.

His Kindness

craft

What You Need
- duplicated page
- envelopes
- hole punch
- stapler
- colored duct tape

What to Do
1. Duplicate and cut out pictures for each child.
2. Cut the flaps off of five envelopes for each child.
3. Allow the children to color the story pictures.
4. Tell the children to glue each picture to a craft stick.
5. Staple each child's four envelopes together at the sides (opening at top). Cover the staples with tape.
6. Show how to write the numbers one to four on the envelopes' fronts.
7. Show how to put the correct pictures in the envelopes.
8. Read the story on page 37. Encourage the children to play with the puppets while they "read" the story with you.

His Kindness

Kindness in the Temple

Chapter 5
I Praise Jesus for His Love

 **Memory Verse**

I have loved you.
John 15:9 CEV

Story to Share
Hold Me, Jesus

Jesus was very different from the other religious leaders, who cared more about how they looked and acted than about the love in their hearts. Those who heard Jesus preach and watched Him work miracles loved Him immediately. Even when He spoke about something that was difficult for the people to hear, Jesus' eyes were filled with love.

The people knew that Jesus thought children were important, too. So these parents decided to take their children to Jesus and ask Him to pray for them. But when the disciples saw all the women with their small children, the disciples waved them away.

"Jesus is busy," one of them said. "Don't waste His time."

Jesus heard the disciple. In anger, He said, "Don't ever send children away from Me."

Then Jesus motioned for the children to come nearer.

"See these children?" Jesus asked. "The kingdom of heaven belongs to those who are as willing to believe as these boys and girls do. They are humble, and you will need their kind of humility to enter heaven."

Then Jesus stretched out His arms and hugged the children to Him. He laughed when He heard a tiny girl say, "Hug me, Jesus, hug me."

Jesus hugged them all. He whispered, "I love you" in their ears, and He tickled them until they giggled.

The parents smiled. They knew this was one day the boys and girls would never forget. They would always feel Jesus' arms of love around them.

— Based on Mark 10:13-16

Discussion Questions

1. Did Jesus want to hug the children? (yes)
2. How does Jesus hug us today? (through our parents, through the warm, safe feelings we have)

craft

What You Need
• duplicated page
• florist tape
• craft sticks
• glue
• curling ribbon

What to Do
1. Duplicate and cut out a daisy for each child.
2. Precut curling ribbon in 12" lengths, three per child. Curl the ends.
3. Give each child two daisies. Show how to glue the daisies back to back on a craft stick.
4. Assist each child in wrapping florist tape around the craft stick to make the daisy's stem.
5. Give each child three curled ribbon pieces and assist in tying them around each craft stick's top.
6. Sing the song to the tune of "Mary Had a Little Lamb." Let the children wave their daisy sticks while they sing.

His Love

He Loves Me

Jesus loves me – yes, He does!
Yes, He does. Yes, He does.
Jesus loves me – yes, He does!
He gave me a smile.

Jesus loves you – yes, He does!
Yes, He does. Yes, He does.
Jesus loves you – yes, He does!
He'll give you a smile.

"He loves me, he loves me not" is a game that people play by pulling petals from daises. But when we think of Jesus, we don't need to pull the petals from the daisies. We don't have to wonder if Jesus loves us. We know He does!

Find the Shadow

puzzle

What You Need
- duplicated page
- crayons

What to Do
1. Duplicate a worksheet for each child.
2. Instruct the children to draw a line from the picture to its shadow.

What to Say
Each one of us is different, so our shadows are different. But there's one thing we can have the same: Jesus loves us all! Turn to the child next to you and find something that is different about that person. (Joshua) says (Alexander) is different because he (has brown hair and Joshua's hair is blond). Now let's say together, "Jesus loves us all!"

His Love

craft

What You Need
- duplicated page
- paint, markers or crayons
- scissors

What to Do
1. Duplicate and cut out a heart for each child.
2. Allow the children to decorate their hearts in any way they wish.
3. Assist the children in cutting their hearts in half.
4. Have each child keep half of a heart. Put the other halves in a bag. Allow each child to choose a heart half from the bag.

What to Say
When you find the friend who has the heart to match the one you chose, give him or her a big hug and say, "Jesus loves you, and so do I!"

His Love

Sharing the Love of Jesus

50

Sprinkled with Love

Jesus loves you!

You are sweet!

I ❤ you!

You make me ☺.

You are kind.

You are a good friend.

Continued from right...

to decorate their baskets with heart stickers.

6. Give the children the message hearts and some candy hearts. Encourage the children to share their hearts and candy with others.

What to Say

You can sprinkle love by sharing what you have in your basket. When you have shared them all, you will be able to read the secret heart in the bottom of your basket.

snack

What You Need
- duplicated page
- applesauce cups
- spoons
- strawberry gelatin mix
- heart stickers
- candy message hearts
- paper fasteners
- poster board

What to Do
1. Cut poster board into 6" x 1" strips. Duplicate and cut out a set of message hearts for each child.
2. Give each child an applesauce cup. Allow the children to sprinkle "love" (gelatin mix) on their sauce, mix and enjoy!
3. Wash the applesauce cups. Assist each child in attaching a handle to his or her cup with a poster board strip and two paper fasteners to form a basket.
4. Give each child a "Jesus Loves You" heart to glue to the bottom of his or her basket.
5. Allow the children
   Continued at left...

His Love

activity

What You Need
- duplicated page and page 87
- crayons
- hook and loop tape
- flannel board

What to Do
1. Duplicate Jesus, then color and cut out the pattern. Attach a piece of the stiff side of hook and loop tape to the back.
2. Duplicate a boy for each boy and a girl for each girl.
3. Let the children color the pictures. Provide hook and loop tape for the back of each one. Help print the child's name on the picture.
4. Place Jesus on the board. Tell the Bible story.
5. Say, "There was probably a boy who had (big blue eyes) like (Ethan) who came to Jesus." Continue with all the children. Allow each child to put his or her picture on the board.

His Love

Verse Rebus

 have

 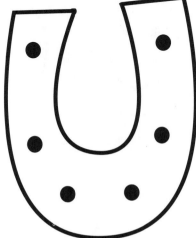

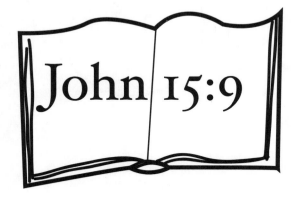

John 15:9

What You Need
- duplicated page
- card stock
- hole punch
- large wiggle eyes
- red tissue paper
- chenille stems
- red ribbon
- alphabet cereal
- plastic sandwich bags

What to Do
1. Duplicate a verse set to card stock for each child. Cut out each piece in the set.
2. Punch holes around the "U" where indicated.
3. Give the children "h-a-v-e" cereal letters to glue on the word "have."
4. Instruct the children to glue the wiggle eye to the eye, and then glue the tissue paper to the heart.
5. Give the children chenille stems to lace in and out of the "U" holes. Assist in cutting off the excess.
6. Allow the children

Continued at left...

Continued from right...

to glue the ribbon to the Bible center.
7. For each child, place his or her set of pieces in a bag to take home.
8. Explain to the children what each piece of the memory verse means. Ask, "Who said these words?" (Jesus)
9. When the children can put the verse in order, ask them to close their eyes and put the verse in order by feeling it.

What to Say

Even when your eyes are closed at night, Jesus loves you and will watch over you. He will always love you!

His Love

game

What You Need
• duplicated page
• crayons

What to Do
1. Duplicate and cut out a game board and nine smile disks for each child.
2. Have each child select six crayons.
3. Allow the children to color the sad faces on the game board, each one in a different color of their six crayons. Instruct them to color their smile disks in different colors also.
4. Allow the children to cover the sad faces with the same color of happy faces.

What to Say
How do you think the children felt when the disciples sent them away from Jesus? (sad) What did their sad faces turn into when Jesus wanted to hug them? (happy faces)

Continued on next page...

His Love

Sad to Glad Color Match

I have loved you. John 15:9

Love Wiggle Buster

game

What You Need
- duplicated page
- marker
- assorted stickers
- small safety pins

What to Do
1. Duplicate a nametag for each child.
2. Print each child's name on a tag.
3. Allow the children to choose their favorite stickers and attach them to their tags.
4. Pin the tags on the children.
5. Say the poem for the children, instructing them to call out their names after "My name is." Encourage the children to do the motions in the poem.
6. When everyone is seated, pray a short prayer, thanking Jesus for His love which He gives to everyone.

His Love

Your name is (Kate)
And you're very special.
Jesus gave you love,
And now your heart is full.

Soooo…

Stand up straight,
Head up high.
Clap your hands,
Now a big sigh.

My name is
_____
and
Jesus loves
me!

Shrug your shoulders.
Wiggle your toes.
Hug yourself,
And wiggle your nose.

Nod your head.
Stomp your feet.
We'll thank Jesus for His love
When you take your seat!

Chapter 6
I Praise Jesus for His Comfort

 ## Memory Verse

He will show compassion.
Lamentations 3:32

 ## Story to Share
Jesus Cries with His Friends

Whenever Jesus was in the village of Bethany, He stayed at the home of his dear friends Lazarus, Mary and Martha. Martha always provided wonderful meals for Jesus and His disciples. It was a place Jesus could relax and just enjoy being with His friends.

One day, Lazarus became very ill. Mary and Martha knew only Jesus could heal him. They sent word for Jesus to come quickly. But before Jesus arrived, Lazarus died.

The sisters grieved loudly. They wrapped Lazarus in linen cloths. They wrapped a linen square around his head. Mary tucked aloe and myrrh between the folds of the linen. They spared no expense in burying their dear brother.

When Jesus finally arrived, Martha ran to Him.

"Jesus, you should have come sooner," she said. "If you would have been here, Lazarus wouldn't have died."

Jesus saw the pain in Martha's eyes. Then He saw Mary sobbing in grief. His heart ached for His friends, and Jesus cried with them.

Then Jesus raised His head and asked, "Where have you taken Lazarus?"

The sisters led Him to the cave where the tomb was.

"Take away the stone," Jesus told some of the men nearby.

After the stone was rolled away, Jesus called, "Lazarus, arise!"

Everyone gasped in astonishment as they saw Lazarus, his head and body still wound tightly in the linen, walking toward Jesus' voice. Jesus had brought Lazarus back to life!

— Based on John 11:1-44

❓❓ Discussion Questions

1. Why did Jesus cry? (He was sorry His friends were hurting.)
2. How does Jesus comfort us when we are hurting? (through a mother's kisses and daddy's hugs, through friends who care for us, through promises in God's Word)

song

What You Need
- duplicated page
- crayons
- wiggle eyes
- dessert-size paper plates
- dry beans
- stapler
- paint stirrers
- tape
- glue

What to Do
1. Duplicate a sad and a happy face for each child.
2. Allow the children to color the faces and glue on the wiggle eyes.
3. Give each child two plates. Instruct each child to glue a face on the back of each paper plate.
4. Assist each child in placing a handful of beans in one plate and stapling the other on top, sandwiching the paint stirrer in-between. Cover the staples with clear tape to prevent injury.
5. Allow the children to play their noisemakers,

Continued at right...

His Comfort

Sad and Happy Noisemakers

I'm a little sad now.
I have cried.
My brother was sick and then he died.
Mary, my sweet sister, is crying, too.
What, oh, what should we do?

Now my heart is happy.
I've got a smile.
Jesus came to see us and cried awhile.
Then He raised my brother from the dead.
"Come forth, Laz," is what He said.

Continued from left...
turning the plates to the correct face as you sing the "Jesus Helps Me Smile" song to the tune of "I'm a Little Teapot."

Musical Comfort

Jesus cares when I am sad,
If I hurt or just feel bad.
When I tell Him all my woes,
I can feel the love He shows.

Yes, Jesus cares.
Yes, Jesus cares.
Yes, Jesus cares.
I feel His presence near.

What You Need
• duplicated page
• construction paper

What to Do
1. Use the pattern to cut hearts out of various colors of construction paper. Cut out tears to match.
2. Place chairs in a circle. Attach a heart to the back of each chair.
3. Give each child a colored tear. Sing the "Jesus Cares" song to the tune of "Jesus Loves Me." Instruct the children to match their tears to hearts and sit down as the song is sung.

What to Say
What makes you sad? You can tell Jesus, and He will comfort your heart.

His Comfort

craft

What You Need

- duplicated page
- crayons
- hole punch
- cotton balls
- potpourri oil
- glue
- thread

What to Do

1. Duplicate a party hat front and back for each child.
2. Allow the children to color their party hats.
3. Assist the children in punching holes where indicated.
4. Give each child four cotton balls with a drop of oil on each one. Instruct the children to glue the cotton balls between the two party hats, folding over the side and gluing to secure.
5. Tie a length of thread through the holes for hanging.

His Comfort

Verse Room Freshener

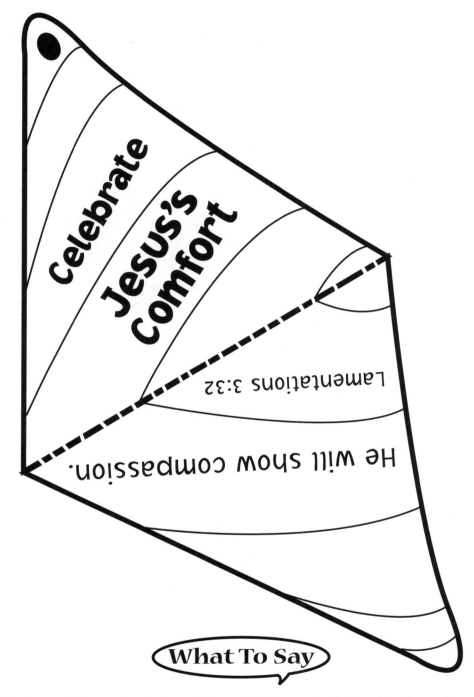

Celebrate Jesus's Comfort

Lamentations 3:32

He will show compassion.

What To Say

Martha and Mary placed aloe and myrrh between the folds of the linen they wrapped around Lazarus. Your party hat should make your room smell good. When you smell the scent, remember to celebrate Jesus' comfort. He showed compassion to Mary and Martha. He will show compassion to you, too.

Patchwork Comfort Card

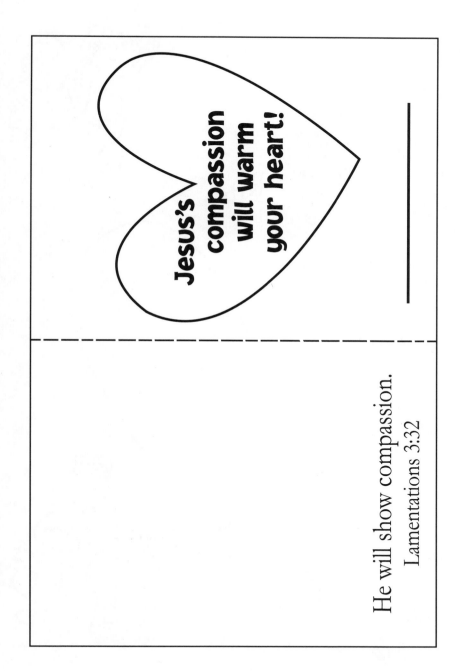

Jesus's compassion will warm your heart!

He will show compassion.
Lamentations 3:32

craft

What You Need
- duplicated page
- 1" fabric squares
- glue

What to Do
1. Duplicate a card for each child.
2. Give each child some fabric squares to glue on the front of the card to resemble a quilt.
3. Assist the children in printing their names on the lines inside their cards.
4. Arrange to take the children to a care facility for the elderly. Or gather the cards and deliver them. Be sure to take pictures of the elderly with the cards to show the children.

What to Say
When you are sick or sad you probably like to cuddle up in a warm blanket. Jesus' comfort can be like putting a quilt on your heart. It makes you feel warm and loved!

His Comfort

puzzle

What You Need
• duplicated page
• crayons

What to Do
1. Duplicate a worksheet for each child.
2. Discuss the pictures on the worksheet.
3. Instruct the children to color the pictures that show compassion. Allow them to draw a red "X" through the pictures that do not show compassion.
4. Assist the children who need help to print their names in the hearts.

What to Say
Sometimes Jesus uses us to give comfort. Can you see someone in the pictures giving comfort? If you want Jesus to use you, take your red crayon and color the heart in the middle of the page. Now print your name in the heart.

His Comfort

Giving Comfort Worksheet

Story People

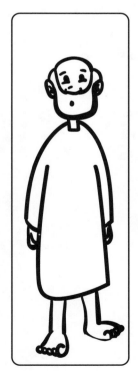

craft

What You Need
- duplicated page
- crayons
- gauze, cut in ½" strips
- spring-type clothespins
- potpourri, crushed fine
- glue

What to Do
1. Duplicate and cut out a story people set for each child.
2. Allow the children to color the story pictures.
3. Give each child a piece of gauze to wrap around Lazarus. Show how to sprinkle some potpourri between the wrappings.
4. Help the children glue the story pictures on the clothespins.
5. Make a story people set to tell the Bible story. After the children have made their own sets, allow them to take turns telling the story to each other.

His Comfort

craft

What You Need
• duplicated page
• crayons
• ribbon curls
• confetti
• glue
• construction paper
• yarn

What to Do
1. Duplicate a poster for each child.
2. Pre-cut ribbon in 3" pieces and curl.
3. Give each child a poster. Instruct the children to trace the words with crayons, using a different color for each word.
4. Allow the children to glue the ribbon curls and confetti to their posters.
5. Give each child a piece of construction paper to glue to the back of his or her poster. Punch two holes and tie a length of yarn through for hanging.

His Comfort

Verse Poster

I Praise Jesus for His Comfort

He will show compassion.

Lamentations 3:32

Wrapping Lazarus

He will show compassion.

Lamentations 3:32

What You Need
• duplicated page
• small boxes
• gray spray paint
• gray crayons
• flour tortillas
• paper fasteners
• hotdogs, cut in half

What to Do
1. Duplicate a stone for each child. Spray paint the boxes gray. Cut a hole in the side of each box, a bit smaller than the stone.
2. Just before class, warm the hotdogs and cut the tortillas into strips.
3. Allow the children to color the stones gray. Assist in attaching the stones in front of the holes on the boxes.
4. Give each child a hotdog half and a tortilla strip. Explain that the hotdog represents Lazarus and the unrolled tortilla strip the cloth they wrapped around him. Allow the

Continued at left...

Continued from right...
   children to wrap the hotdogs in the cloths.
5. Instruct each child to lay his or her wrapped "Lazarus" in a tomb.
6. Allow the children to say, "Lazarus, arise," and bring their snacks out of their tombs. Slice the hotdogs into small pieces to prevent choking.
7. The tomb also can be used with "Story People" on page 63.

His Comfort

Chapter 7
I Praise Jesus for His Forgiveness

 Memory Verse

He forgave us all our sins.
Colossians 2:13

 Story to Share

Father, Forgive Them

When people sinned, God was sad. He knew the only way their sins could be forgiven was for a sinless man to die in place of them. That's why God sent His Son, Jesus, to earth as a tiny baby. He knew Jesus would grow up and be the sinless man who could die for the sins of all people.

Jesus did many wonderful miracles while He was on earth. He taught about His Father, God. He preached love, forgiveness and joy. He loved everyone, not just the wealthy or beautiful, but also the poor, the disfigured, and even those who hated Him.

One day those men who hated Jesus nailed Him to a cross. They beat Jesus, spat in His face, put thorns on His head like a crown and then put nails through His hands and feet. How Jesus suffered! But the words He spoke remind us how sinless He was.

"Father, forgive them," Jesus prayed as He hung on the cross.

When Jesus died, they put Him in a tomb. His mother, Mary, was sad. His disciples were sad. Those who loved Him and believed He was the Son of God were sad. But they didn't know the secret.

Three days later, Jesus rose from the dead. Soldiers had sealed the stone on the tomb so nobody could steal His body – but that didn't keep Him inside. Jesus rose from the grave and is alive today!

And now, because Jesus died, we can be forgiven from our sins. Jesus wants us to believe He is the Son of God. He wants us to tell Him our sins. Then Jesus is ready to forgive us. He is our Savior.

— Based on Matthew 27:32-28:10

Discussion Questions

1. What did the men do to Jesus that caused Him to ask God to forgive the men? (beat Him, spit on Him, crucified Him)
2. What will Jesus forgive you for? (disobeying, selfishness, unloving attitudes)

puzzle

What You Need
• duplicated patterns
• safety scissors
• glue
• crayons

What to Do
1. Duplicate a worksheet for each child.
2. Allow the children to color and cut out the pictures.
3. Read the words under the pictures, one phrase at a time. Instruct the children to decide whether each picture shows an action Jesus will forgive, then glue the picture to the correct side.

What to Say
Look at all the pictures. They are all on the side of actions Jesus will forgive. Our verse says Jesus will forgive all our sins. Let's say the verse together.

Continued on next page...

His Forgiveness

Forgiveness Worksheet

Sarah stole a candy bar.

Bryan wouldn't share his car with Katie.

Maria told her mother a lie.

Robbie kicked his friend.

Forgiven

He forgave us all our sins.
Colossians 2:13

NOT Forgiven

Cross of Forgiveness

snack

What You Need
- duplicated page
- colored card stock
- clear, self-stick plastic
- graham crackers
- chocolate frosting
- plastic knives
- sprinkles

What to Do
1. Duplicate a place mat to colored card stock for each child. Cover the place mats with self-stick plastic.
2. Give each child a graham cracker broken into fourths.
3. Allow the children to spread the frosting on the crackers.
4. Show how to lay the crackers on a place mat to form a cross.

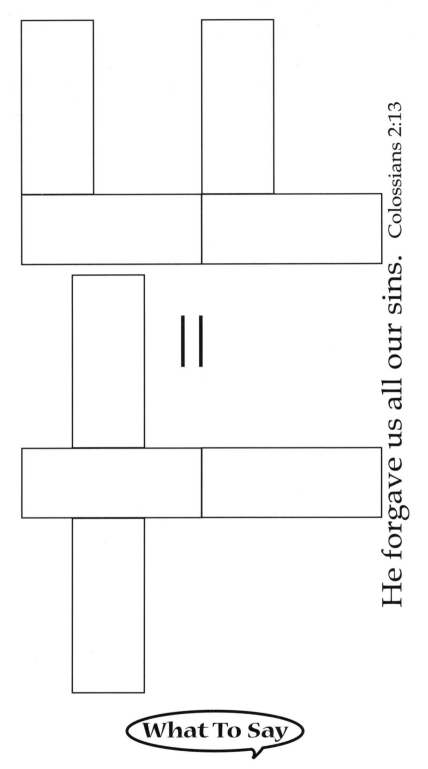

He forgave us all our sins. Colossians 2:13

What To Say

Jesus didn't just die on the cross, He died so we could have the gift of forgiveness. Let's put these sprinkles on our cross to remind us of the extra-special gift Jesus gave to us. The word "forgiveness" begins with an "F." We can turn the cross into the letter "F." Before we eat, let's thank God for our snack and for sending His Son so we can be forgiven from our sins.

His Forgiveness

Forgiveness Song

What You Need
- duplicated page
- crayons
- cross and child stickers

What to Do
1. Duplicate and cut out a songbook for each child.
2. Allow the children to color their songbooks.
3. Help the children print "FORGIVE" on the cover of the songbook.
4. Give each child a cross and child sticker to attach to the front of their books.
5. Sing the song to the tune of "B-I-N-G-O."

He forgave us all our sins.
Colossians 2:13

When someone does
a wrong to me,
I'll do what Jesus did.
F-O-R, Forgive,
F-O-R, Forgive,
F-O-R, Forgive,
I will forgive them, too.

When Jesus died
upon the cross,
He said, "Father, forgive."
F-O-R, Forgive,
F-O-R, Forgive,
F-O-R, Forgive,
"Father, forgive these men."

His Forgiveness

71

craft

What You Need
- duplicated page
- self-stick plastic
- glitter
- heart punch
- colored paper
- ribbon
- water-based marker

What to Do
1. Trace the cross pattern to cardboard for a template.
2. Allow the children to punch hearts from different colors of paper.
3. Give each child two 4" x 8" pieces of clear plastic.
4. Peel the backing from one piece of each child's plastic and place it on the table, sticky side up.
5. Instruct the children to press the colored hearts on the sticky side of the plastic. Assist the children in sprinkling glitter over the hearts.
6. Go around and peel the paper off each child's second square and press

Continued at right...

His Forgiveness

Cross Sun Catcher

Continued from left...
into the first.
7. Using a water-based marker and the cross template, trace a cross on each child's plastic and cut it out.
8. Allow the children to punch holes at the tops of their crosses. Assist the children in tying lengths of ribbon through the crosses for hanging.

What to Say
God gave His Son, Jesus, to die for our sins because He loves us. Jesus was willing to die because He loves us, too. The hearts in your cross will remind you of His love. How can you show your love for God and His Son?

Scene in a Cup

What You Need
- duplicated page
- crayons
- 8-oz. foam cups
- glue
- tiny silk flowers

What to Do
1. Duplicate and cut out a cross circle, tomb and verse for each child.
2. Let the children color the pictures.
3. Assist each child in gluing the circle to the inside bottom of a cup.
4. Show how to fold the tab on the tomb and glue it to the wall of the cup, about halfway in.
5. Have the children glue the verse rectangles on the outsides of the cups.
6. Let the children glue silk flowers near their tombs.

What to Say
Jesus died as a sinless offering for our sins. But not only did He die, He arose from the grave and is living today!

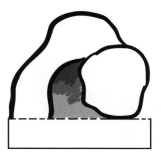

He forgave
us ALL our
sins.
Colossians 2:13

His Forgiveness

activity

What You Need
- duplicated page
- overhead transparency sheets
- paper clip
- dry erase markers
- rags

What to Do
1. Duplicate a cross picture for each child.
2. Clip transparency sheets to the cross pictures.
3. Instruct the children to trace the lines of the picture with markers.
4. When they are finished, unclip the transparencies and hold them up for the children to see.
5. Show the children that they can wipe the transparencies clean with soft rags and trace again.

His Forgiveness

Magic Picture

He forgave us all our sins. Colossians 2:13

I'm Forgiven Wristlet

I'm forgiven!

I'm forgiven!

I'm forgiven!

craft

What You Need
- duplicated page
- crayons
- small stickers
- clear tape

What to Do
1. Duplicate a wristlet for each child.
2. Allow the children to color their wristlets.
3. Give the children small stickers to decorate their wristlets.
4. Fit the wristlet to each child's wrist, fastening with clear tape. Cut off the excess paper.

What to Say
When you wear your I'm Forgiven Wristlet, you will be reminded that Jesus forgives our sins when we ask Him. It will also remind you that Jesus wants us to forgive others.

His Forgiveness

puzzle

What You Need
• duplicated page
• crayons
• scissors

What to Do
1. Duplicate the grid for each child.
2. Give each child a grid and let the children color the pictures.
3. Assist the children who need help cutting the squares apart.

What to Say
Let's find all of our cut-out hearts and place them in a pile. God sent His Son, Jesus, to earth because He loves us.
Let's find our crosses. Jesus died on the cross so our sins could be forgiven.
Let's find our tombs. Jesus arose from the dead. He's alive!
Let's find our praying hands. We can ask Jesus to forgive our sins.
Let's find our party cakes. We can celebrate Jesus's forgiveness.

His Forgiveness

Sort and Learn

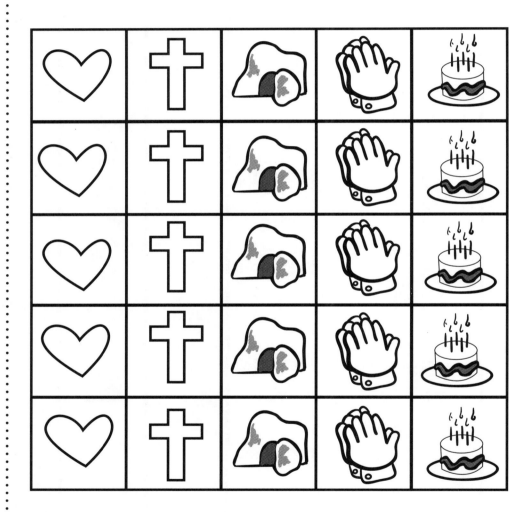

Chapter 8
I Praise Jesus for His Home

 ## Memory Verse

He has prepared a city.
Hebrews 11:16

 ## Story to Share
Living with Jesus

One day while Jesus was teaching His disciples, He told them about heaven.

He said, "Where My Father lives are many mansions. I am going to prepare one for you."

"But wait a minute," Thomas said to Jesus. "Are You saying we have to find our own way to heaven?"

"No," Jesus answered. "I am the way to heaven. If you believe I am the Son of God, then you also know my Father."

The disciples didn't understand what Jesus was saying. But they did know that they believed Jesus was the Son of God.

Soon it was time for Jesus to return to His Father in heaven. The disciples were sad. Jesus was their best Friend. How could they go on without Him?

While the disciples were still looking up to the sky where Jesus had disappeared into the clouds, they heard a voice. Two angels were watching them.

"Don't be sad," the angels told the disciples. "Jesus is coming back one day to take you, and all those who believe He is the Son of God, to heaven with Him."

Later, one disciple, John, had a dream about heaven. He saw thousands and thousands of angels singing praise songs to God. He saw beautiful palaces and golden streets.

The vision made John want to be with Jesus in heaven even more. John knew that heaven would be a perfect place with no sadness or pain. So he spent the rest of his life telling people how wonderful heaven would be. He even wrote a book about it. That book is the last one in the Bible. It is called "Revelation."

— Based on John 14:1-14, Acts 1:1-11, Revelation

Discussion Questions

1. What do you think heaven is like? (beautiful, shiny, angels, fun)
2. How can you be ready for heaven? (believe Jesus is God's Son and confess your sins)

Finish the Picture

puzzle

What You Need
- duplicated page
- crayons

What to Do
1. Duplicate a worksheet for each child.
2. Explain to the children that the picture of heaven seems to be missing a few important things. Name the missing pieces one by one and allow time for the children to fill them in, then allow the children to color their pictures.

What to Say
Draw a roof on the mansion with a brown crayon. Draw water in the river with a blue crayon. Draw fruit on the tree with a green crayon. Draw wings on the angel with a yellow crayon. Draw a smile on the child with a red crayon.

His Home

He has prepared a city. Hebrews 11:16

78

Heavenly Clouds

He has prepared a city. Hebrews 11:16

snack

What You Need
- duplicated page
- crayons
- glitter glue
- marshmallow cream
- 8-oz. cream cheese
- wax paper
- toothpicks
- cut fruit

What to Do
1. Duplicate a place card for each child.
2. Make the dip by mixing the cream cheese with a jar of marshmallow cream.
3. Allow the children to color their cards.
4. Assist the children in printing their names on the lines.
5. Instruct the children to add some glitter glue to the "Son rays." Explain that in heaven, the light comes not from the sun as it does now, but from Jesus.
6. Give each child a wax paper square with cut fruit and three clouds of dip. Allow the children to use the toothpicks and fruit to build "mansions in the clouds."

His Home

song

What You Need
• duplicated page
• cotton balls
• glitter glue
• yellow or gold crayons

What to Do
1. Duplicate a heaven picture for each child.
2. Allow the children to color their pictures and add glitter glue to the light rays.
3. Give the children cotton balls to stretch out and glue on the clouds.
4. Form a circle with the children. Sing the song to the tune of "The Hokey Pokey." Instruct the children to hold up their pictures of heaven when they shout at the end.

Shoutin' Heaven

I'll put my happy self in,
I'll put my happy self out,
I'll put my happy self in,
And I'll hop all about.
I'm gonna go to heaven and see my Jesus there,
That makes me want to shout. (HEAVEN!)

He has prepared a city. Hebrews 11:16

His Home

Traveling to Heaven

Grandma's	Outside	Heaven

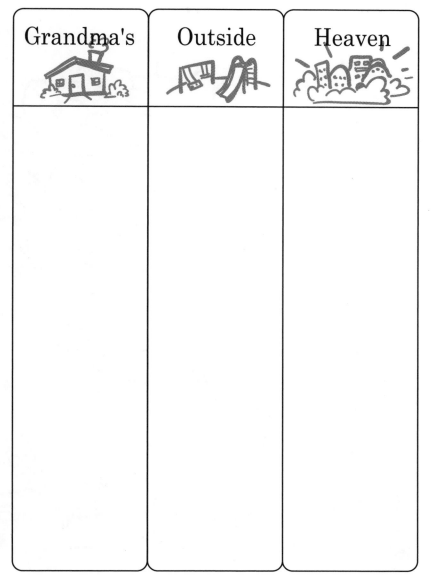

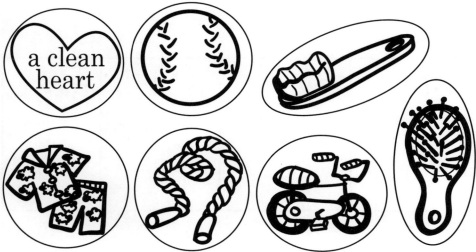

puzzle

What You Need
- duplicated page
- crayons
- scissors
- glue

What to Do
1. Duplicate a worksheet for each child.
2. Allow the children to color and cut out the pictures.
3. Instruct the children to find three things they need if they are going to grandma's house and glue them under the grandma picture.
4. Instruct the children to find three things they need if they are going to play outside and glue them under the park picture.

What to Say
There's one thing left: a clean heart. That's all you need when you go to heaven. Let's glue the heart under the heaven picture.

His Home

Count Them All

What You Need
• duplicated page
• crayons

What to Do
1. Duplicate a worksheet for each child.
2. Allow the children to color the pictures.
3. Ask, "How many houses do you see in the picture of heaven, Jesus's home?" Instruct the children to count the houses.
4. Print the number on the board for the children to copy. Instruct the children to print the number in the square next to the house. Continue with the angels, clouds and flowers.

What to Say
Jesus gave the disciples one command: "Go tell everyone about Me and My gift of salvation." Jesus wants us to tell others about Him, too. How many people can you tell about Jesus?

His Home

What's in Heaven?

Jesus Goes Home

craft

What You Need
- duplicated pages
- crayons
- yarn
- tape

What to Do
1. Duplicate and cut out a scene picture and a Jesus picture for each child.
2. Cut slits on the dashed lines on the pictures.
3. Allow the children to color the pictures.
4. Assist each child in taping a Jesus to a length of yarn and threading the yarn through the slits, pulling tight. Tape the ends together.
5. Show how to pull the yarn on the back of the picture to move Jesus toward His home.

Continued on next page...

His Home

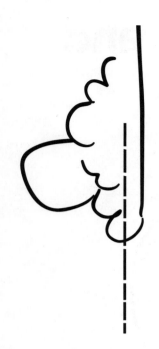

craft

What You Need
- duplicated page
- card stock
- craft foam
- chenille stems
- markers
- hole punch

What to Do
1. Duplicate the eyeglasses pattern once to card stock for tracing.
2. Using the card stock pattern, cut foam eyeglasses for each child. Punch a hole in the top of each corner.
3. Allow the children to decorate their glasses with markers.
4. Instruct each child to twist a chenille stem into each hole. Help them curve the ends like ear pieces. Go around and cut off the excess.
5. Have the children put on their glasses.

Seeing Jesus and His Home

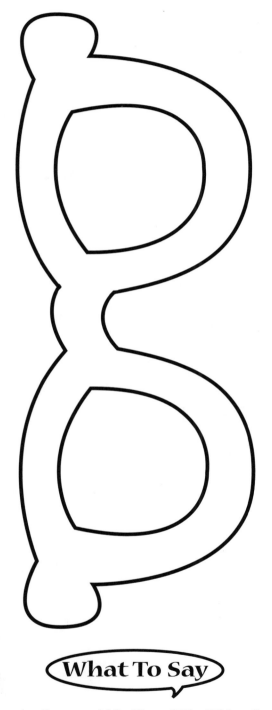

What To Say

Can you imagine seeing Jesus and His Home? The Bible tells us to watch for when He comes back to take us to heaven. We can watch for Jesus by obeying His Word and keeping our hearts free from sin.

His Home

Chapter 9
Miscellaneous

activity

What You Need
- duplicated page
- party hats
- hook and loop tape
- crayons

What to Do
1. Duplicate a set of story icons for each child.
2. Put a 1″ piece of hook tape on the front of each party hat.
3. Allow the children to color the story icon that goes with the lesson.
4. Put a 1″ piece of loop tape on the back of each icon. Attach the icon to the hats for the children to wear.
5. Put the icons in envelopes for the children to take home with their hats at the end of the series.

What to Say
Today we are praising Jesus for [His example]. Wear you party hat to help us praise Him.

Praise Hats

example

home

peace

love

miracles

kind

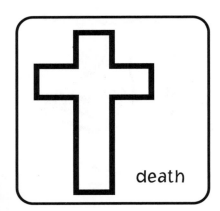

death

forgiveness

Praise Game

game

What You Need
- duplicated page
- crayons
- dice
- game tokens

What to Do
1. Duplicate a game board for each child.
2. Allow the children to color their game boards.
3. Have each child pair with a friend to play the game.
4. This is a great review game for the praise lesson series. The players take turns rolling the dice and moving the correct number of spaces. If a child lands on a party hat, have him or her tell how that Bible story causes us to praise Jesus.

Miscellaneous

song

What You Need
• duplicated page
• poster board
• bean bag
• music note stickers
• glue

What to Do
1. Duplicate and cut out the song squares.
2. Cut a piece of poster board into a 12" square.
3. Glue the song squares randomly on the poster board square. Decorate with music note stickers.
4. Lay the poster board square on the floor. Give a child the beanbag. Allow the child to throw the beanbag on the poster board. Sing the song on which the bag lands.

Miscellaneous

Pick a Song

Jesus Helps Me Smile *Sad and Happy Noisemakers, page 58*	**Shoutin' Heaven** *page 80*
The Miracle Worker *page 34*	**Celebrate God's Son** *Praise Kazoo, page 9*
Do You Know *Sin No More, page 42*	**Jesus Cares** *Musical Comfort, page 59*
My Rockin' Boat *Rocking In the Storm, page 19*	**He Loves Me** *page 48*
F-O-R-G-I-V-E *Forgiveness Song, page 71*	

It's Your Turn

teacher help

What You Need
- duplicated page
- poster board
- spring-type clothespins
- yarn
- glue
- crayons

What to Do
1. Duplicate a party kid for each child.
2. Cut two 14" circles from poster board. Glue the backs of the circles together, sandwiching a looped 10" length of yarn between them for hanging. In the center of one circle, print "It's Your Turn!"
3. Give each child a party kid to color. Instruct the children to glue their kids to the tops of clothespins.
4. Assist the children in printing their names below the kids on the clothespins.
5. Clip the pins around the circle and hang it near the teaching area. Use the pins to keep track of children's turns.

Miscellaneous

activity

What You Need
- duplicated page
- fluorescent poster board, 9" x 13"
- paint stirrer
- glue dots
- ribbon curls
- stapler

What to Do
1. Duplicate a clock to colored paper.
2. Cut out the clock and glue it to the poster board.
3. Print "It's time to Praise Jesus" on the poster board.
4. Attach the ribbon curls around the clock with glue dots.
5. Staple the paint stirrer to the back of the poster board.
6. Explain to the children that whenever they see the Praise Clock, they should immediately stand to their feet and quote the memory verse with you. Allow the children to yell "I Praise Jesus" after they say the verse.

Miscellaneous

Time to Praise

Supply Letter

Will You Help?

Dear Parents and Friends of our Preschoolers,

We're planning on having a blast while we praise Jesus! If you have any of these items we need for our classroom experience, please share them with us.

- party horns
- paper fasteners
- craft sticks
- large and small wiggle eyes
- plastic icing cans
- plastic bandages
- aluminum foil
- pink felt
- plastic snack bags
- black foam
- letter-size envelopes
- curling ribbon
- colored file folders
- cotton balls
- gauze
- confetti
- spring-type clothespins
- baby food jars
- florist tape

Thank you!

_____
teacher

teacher help

What You Need
- duplicated page

What to Do
1. Duplicate a supply letter for each family in your church. (Even families who do not have children might be happy to help with class materials.)
2. Fold each letter in thirds and seal with a sticker.

Miscellaneous

Verse Holder

craft

What You Need
- duplicated pages
- plastic drinking straws
- tape
- glue
- dessert-size paper plates
- crayons

What to Do
1. Duplicate and cut out a Jesus circle and verse party hat set for each child.
2. Following the rim curve of the paper plate, cut one 3" slit at the top and one at the bottom of the rim.
3. Assist the children in printing their names on the lines of their Jesus circles.
4. Allow the children to color their Jesus circles and glue them to the center of their plates.
5. Punch a hole at the top of each paper plate and attach a piece of yarn for hanging. Hang the plates at child height so a verse can be added

Continued on next page...

Miscellaneous

is praising Jesus

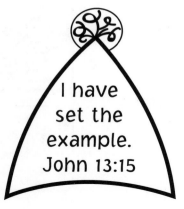
I have
set the
example.
John 13:15

My peace
I give you.
John 14:27

See Jesus
do a miracle.
Mark 3:10

The Lord
is good.
Lamentations 3:25

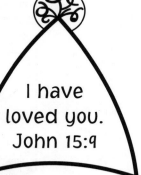
I have
loved you.
John 15:9

He will
show
compassion.
Lamentations 3:32

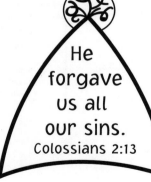
He
forgave
us all
our sins.
Colossians 2:13

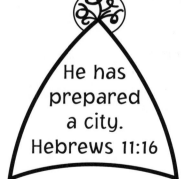
He has
prepared
a city.
Hebrews 11:16

craft

Continued from previous page...
each week.

6. Allow the children to color each lesson's verse hat as you get to that lesson.

7. Tape a straw to the back of each hat. Allow each child to stick his or her verse hat in the holder (top of straw in top slit and bottom in bottom slit) when that child can quote the verse.

Miscellaneous

Apron Review

What You Need
- duplicated images from page 88
- kitchen apron or construction apron
- felt
- double-stick tape
- clothespins

What to Do

1. Duplicate and cut out the review pictures on page 88. Color the pictures.
2. Cut felt into 5" squares.
3. Attach the felt squares to an apron with double-stick tape to form pockets.
4. Slide a picture in each pocket, leaving portion of the pictures sticking out of the tops of the pockets.
5. Allow a child to pull a picture out of a pocket then attach it to the front of your apron with a clothespin. Ask a simple review question for the child to answer.

Miscellaneous

His Example:
In which town was Jesus born? (Bethlehem)
What was Jesus' bed? (A manger)

His Peace:
Where were the disciples when the storm came? (in a boat)
What was Jesus doing? (sleeping)

His Miracles:
What did Jesus do to the man who couldn't hear? (He healed the man's ears.)
What was in the little boy's lunch that fed so many people? (five loaves and two fish)

His Kindness:
Why did the men want to throw stones at the woman? (She sinned.)
What did Jesus say? (If you have never sinned, you can throw a stone.)

His Love:
What were the disciples telling the children? (Go away! Jesus is busy.)
Was Jesus happy that the disciples sent the children away? (No, Jesus gathered them around Him.)

His Comfort:
Which friend of Jesus' died? (Lazarus)
Who were Lazarus's sisters? (Mary and Martha)

His Forgiveness:
To what did the men nail Jesus? (a cross)
What did Jesus do to these men? (He forgave them.)

His Home:
Where did Jesus go when He went home? (Heaven)
Who told the disciples Jesus was coming back? (angels)